At the Rebbe's Table

Rabbi Zalman Schachter-Shalomi's
Legacy of Songs and Melodies
Volume II

At the Rebbe's Table

Rabbi Zalman Schachter-Shalomi's
Legacy of Songs and Melodies
Volume II

Collected, Transcribed
& Edited by

Eyal Rivlin
& Netanel Miles-Yepez

With Contributions by
Hazzan Richard Kaplan

Albion
Andalus
The Jewish Renewal Series
Boulder, Colorado
2012

"The old shall be renewed,
and the new shall be made holy."
— Rabbi Avraham Yitzhak Kook

Original musical interpretations by Zalman Schachter-Shalomi

Copyright © 2011 Zalman Schachter-Shalomi

Original musical transcriptions and text for *Into My Garden*

Copyright © 2011 Eyal Rivlin and Netanel Miles-Yepez

Albion-Andalus, Inc.
P. O. Box 19852
Boulder, CO 80308
www.albionandalus.com

Design and composition by Albion-Andalus, Inc.
Cover design by Daryl McCool, D.A.M. Cool Graphics
Cover photo by Surya Green.

Manufactured in the United States of America

ISBN-10: 1453874747
ISBN-13: 978-1453874745

Contents

In remembrance of my father, Shlomo HaKohen
Schachter, and my friends, Barukh Merzel,
Shlomo Carlebach, and Max Helfman

— Zalman Schachter-Shalomi

In honor of my grandfathers,
Shalom Dror and Ben-Ami Rivlin,
who have sown the seeds of *niggun* within me.

— Eyal Rivlin

For the Rebbe's many heirs, who will continue to sing
these *niggunim* for generations to come.

— Netanel Miles-Yepez

Acknowledgements

WE WISH TO OFFER our heartfelt thanks and enduring gratitude to our beloved *rebbe*, Reb Zalman, who so joyously kept remembering more and more melodies, and whose excitement about this project has made it a joy to work on. Special thanks are due to: Hazzan Richard Kaplan, who first began collecting and transcribing these *niggunim* many years ago, and who is directly responsible for "Hokhmat Adam Tair Panav," the "D'veiqut Niggun," and "Yah Ekhsof Noam Shabbat" as they are transcribed in this volume; Hazzan Robert Michael Esformes who contributed his own ideas at the initial stage of this project; Neilah Carlebach, for permission to use the music for "Lord I Want to Do for You"; Sigmond Kal Shore, for permission to tell the story of his encounter with the Pope; and Mary Fulton, who always knows which computer does what, and who skillfully helped us locate and gather any pre-existing material. Others to whom we are grateful include: Daryl McCool of D.A.M. Cool Graphics for the cover design; Sheldon Sands for engineering the recording sessions in his studio with heart and skill; Joe Lukasik for checking the transcriptions against the music; the Archives of the University of Colorado at Boulder for use of the photos of the Zalman M. Schachter-Shalomi Collection; and finally, a big thank you to the amazing board of the Yesod Foundation (Ron Claman, David Friedman, Tirzah Firestone, Thomas Hast and Bobbie Zelkind) whose early support helped to make possible the first spiral-bound version of this book (with accompanying CD) by the Reb Zalman Legacy Project.

— E.R. and N.M-Y.

9

Preface to
Volumes I & II

THESE BOOKS are an attempt to answer a question once put to me by Reb Zalman—a *koan* by a Jewish *kohen*. It was the Fall of 2000 and my first semester at Naropa University in Boulder, Colorado. Despite my heavily secular and suspicious Israeli upbringing, I felt drawn to take Reb Zalman's course on Judaism. In one of our first classes, someone asked him, "What is Judaism?" He paused for a moment, closed his eyes, and then started nodding and smiling. He opened his eyes again and answered, "Perhaps the question is not 'What is Judaism?' but rather, 'How do you Jew?'"

That was the 'permission' I had been seeking for many years, allowing me to ask, "How do *I* Jew?" I began to ask myself this question over and over; it wasn't how I *should* or *shouldn't* Jew, but how do I naturally and authentically get closer to God? I am still answering that question, and will probably continue to do so for as long as I live. Nevertheless, one thing is clear: one of my own deepest channels to God is through music, which allows me to both lose myself and find my Self in the melodies.

For me, music is at the core of every religion. Truthfully, I can find as much bliss in chanting Sanskrit mantras as I can rocking-out to old '60's tunes; and yet, the haunting melodies of the Jewish tradition and their Hebrew phrases strike a different chord in my being—a deeper, more cellular (perhaps *soul-ular*) chord, grooved and etched into my DNA over the millennia.

As these *niggunim*, or 'melodies' begin, I feel myself transported—it is as if I am a Levite in the holy Temple, or a Hasid singing with every blade of grass outside the *shtetl*. There is a saying in Hebrew, *shetaltem niggunim bi imi v'avi*, "You have sown the seeds of melodies within me, my ancestors." When I hear these melodies it is as if I've heard them before, and I get that familiar, 'oh yes' feeling. And when I've been present as Reb Zalman sings them himself, I know that I am in the presence of a man *Jew-ing* fully, and I get more in touch with how I can *Jew*.

In these two volumes, we have tried to give you a taste of Reb Zalman's own Jew-bilations, of how he Jews through music. Volume I contains original songs and melodies composed by Reb Zalman and his father, Shlomo HaKohen Schachter, while Volume II contains the Hasidic melodies he remembers hearing and singing before the Holocaust in Europe (some of which perhaps only a handful of people alive today can still recall), as well as those classics that he uses in his teaching.

Louis Armstrong once said, "If you need to ask what Jazz is, you'll never know!" Similarly, I believe that to really *get* the melodies in this book, you need to experience a Hasid like Reb Zalman singing them, and thus we have produced an accompanying CD for each volume, with Reb Zalman singing the melodies himself. Most were recorded specifically for the CDs, but a few were recorded previously for a collection called, *Le Chayim: To Life*.

On a musical note, these songs were often composed and sung extemporaneously without instrumental accompaniment, and thus, I have added simple chords to the transcribed melodies in order to make them more accessible for musicians who might want to use them in their own spiritual communities.

Feel free to adapt and add your own *midrash* (interpretation) to my suggestions.

Also, I have never heard Reb Zalman sing these *niggunim* twice in exactly the same way; therefore, the transcriptions given here are only approximations of primary musical motifs and may differ slightly from the recordings. Finally, the melodies have been transcribed into simple keys for ease of playing, and hence, are often not in the original keys Reb Zalman sings them. Wherever possible, I have tried to indicate this below the transcription.

Even as this book was being prepared for its first printing, I was still receiving calls from Reb Zalman saying, "*Oy!* I just remembered another *niggun!*" He would then record it on his iPod, palm pilot, or digital recorder, and pass a copy to me. So I have a feeling we will continue to uncover and preserve many more of Reb Zalman's musical gems and jams in the future.

May this book inspire and expand your ways of *Jew-ing;* may the melodies of pre-Holocaust Europe continue to be sung; and may Reb Zalman's prayerful spirit continue to shine through his music.

With *Shir* Joy . . .

Eyal Rivlin
Boulder, Colorado

THERE ARE MANY kinds of songs. There are songs I sing when I am doing work, whose purpose is to keep me in the rhythm. There are songs I perform for an audience, whose purpose is to entertain. So the question is—"Why? And for whom are you singing?" For a Hasid, the answer is always "God."

In 1974, the year before I left Winnipeg, there was a performance in the big concert hall there of the sacred service, Avodat HaKodesh *for baritone, choir, and orchestra by the composer, Ernest Bloch. The conductor asked me to bring a* Sefer Torah *to the concert hall. It was on Friday night and they had a double choir and a harp and trumpets, and at one point I came in with the Torah, opened it and read in English. In my mind, I wasn't performing for the audience, I was performing for* HaShem!

When you sing a sacred melody, closing your eyes is an important part of creating intimacy with God. At other times you might want to sing to a Shiviti. *Of course, in some settings neither of these may be necessary. A* niggun *(melody) is a* shir ha'ma'alot, *a 'song of ascension.' As the* niggun *builds and gets stronger, we get closer to God . . . It lifts us up!*

— Zalman Schachter-Shalomi, 2006

Section I
Melodies and Songs of Galician Hasidism

Reb Zalman's father, Shlomo HaKohen Schachter
as a young Belzer Hasid in 1915.

THIS FIRST SELECTION of Galician melodies probably represent the first melodies to which young Zalman Schachter was exposed as a child growing up in Vienna in the late 1920s and 30s. The descendant of a long line of Belzer Hasidism from Galicia, he learned many of these melodies from his father, a Belzer Hasid, and perhaps from the other Galician Hasidim with whom his father associated.

Menuha Ve'Simha Tish*

Syllabic Vocals & Lyrics: (Variable/Hebrew) *Menuha Ve'Simha*.
Source: Shlomo HaKohen Schachter, Vienna, Austria, ca. 1930s.
Origin: Poss. Galicia (Traditional).

'Rest and Joy'

THIS *TISH* (table) *niggun* was sung almost every Friday evening in Reb Zalman's childhood home by his

---

* Original key is Abm (one half step lower, tune guitar down ½ step).

father, Shlomo, for *Shabbat*. It is most likely Galician in origin and may also be sung with the words of *Barukh El Eliyon* as part of the *Shabbat* celebration. Both *Menuha Ve'Simha* and *Barukh El Eliyon* are found in the *Siddur* (prayer-book).

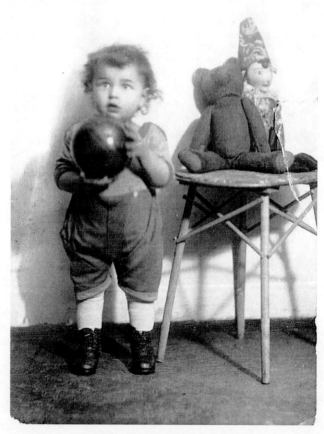

Meshullam Zalman Schachter, ca. 1926.

Mayim Rabim·

Lyrics: (Hebrew) *Shir HaShirim* 8:7,6, added by Zalman Schachter.
Composer: Yosef Hayyim Schachter, Galicia, 19th Century.
Source: Shlomo HaKohen Schachter, Vienna, Austria, ca. 1930s.

---

* Written in its original key (no capo needed).

'Many Waters'

THIS IS A Belzer *niggun* composed by Reb Zalman's great-grandfather, Yosef Hayyim Schachter, a *shohet* (kosher slaughterer) of good reputation and a Belzer Hasid. Though the *niggun* is still sung among Beler Hasidim, this is the version that has come down through the family tradition. Of it, Reb Zalman says:

> This was my great-grandfather's *niggun*, which was originally set to words from the liturgy, from the place where the congregation prays for the cantor so that he might serve them well. In English, this prayer was called, "Please be with the mouth of those who have been sent as ambassadors for your people, Israel." But since the cantor now sings this prayer instead of the congregation and has set it to different music, I took my grandfather's *niggun* and set it to words from the *Song of Songs* so that it could to be used more freely. The more recent Belzer *niggunim* are different from the original Belz, which was very low and meditative, like this *niggun* by my grandfather.

In English, the lyrics from the *Song of Songs* (8:7,6) say:

Many waters cannot quench love,

Nor can the floods drown it;

Set me as a seal upon your heart,

As a seal upon your arm;

For love is as strong as death,

Jealousy is as cruel as hell;
The coals thereof are coals of fire,
Which have a vehement flame.

HaMa'avir Banav*

Syllabic Vocals: (Variable).
Source: Shlomo HaKohen Schachter, Vienna, Austria, ca. 1930s.
Origin: A *niggun* of the Belzer Hasidim.

'He Who Caused His Children To Pass Through the Sea'

THIS *NIGGUN* was originally used by the Belzer Hasidim for the seventh night of *Pesah* (Passover), but is now used on *Simhat Torah*.

A few years ago, while in Israel for his son Barya's wedding, Reb Zalman visited the Belzer Synagogue in Jerusalem, and later described the visit to us:

> The Belzer Hasidim didn't want to let me in at first because I wasn't wearing the Belzer outfit;

---

* Written in its original key (no capo needed).

so I started to talk about *niggunim* with them . . . "Do you know this *niggun?*"

"Yeah sure we know that *niggun.*"

So I said, "That's my great-grandfather's *niggun.*"

Then they made lots of hub-bub, "*Oy! Oy! Oy!*" and in the end, took me downstairs to the office and stuck me in front of a tape recorder. I sang for them some of the Belzer songs I had learned growing up, and when I sang this one, *HaMa'avir Banav*, "the one who causes the children to cross over the sea," their eyes went wide and they said, "That's the *niggun* we use for *hakofes!*"

Belzer Dance·

Syllabic Vocals: (Variable).
Source: Shlomo HaKohen Schachter, Vienna, Austria, ca. 1930s.
Origin: A *niggun* of the Belzer Hasidim.

IN JIRI LANGER'S *Nine Gates to the Chassidic Mysteries*, he describes his first visit to the Galician town of Belz and the Belzer synagogue:

> Small towns in eastern Galicia have all had the same character for centuries. Misery and dirt are their characteristic outward signs. Poorly clad Ukrainian peasant men and women, Jews wearing side-whiskers, in torn caftans, rows of cattle and horses, geese and large pigs grazing

---

* Original key F#m (capo 2). This dance may be used for any occasion.

undisturbed on the square. Belz is distinguished from other places only by its famous synagogue, its no less famous House of Study and the large house belonging to the town rabbi. These three buildings enclose the square on three sides. They are simply constructed. But in this poor, out-of-the-way region of the world they are truly memorable.

He continues a little later:

The spacious Belz synagogue has meanwhile filled with people. There are a hundred lighted candles. In a way the interior reminds me of the Old-New Synagogue in Prague. The men, for the most part tall and well-built, old and young, await the arrival of the rabbi, talking quietly among themselves. In contrast to their weekday appearance, they are all absolutely clean. Their festive caftans of black silk reach down to the ground. On their heads the older ones wear *shtreimels*, which smell of the perfumed tobacco they carry in their tobacco pouches. Some are from Hungary, others from far away—from Russia. Owing to the bad state of the roads they have journeyed for weeks on end to get to Belz, and it may be that they will not be staying there more than a single day. The next day, Sunday, they will set out again on the wearisome journey home.[1]

Reb Zalman's own visit to the Belzer Hasidim in Jerusalem shows a different Belz, but one that is still familiar. Gone is the Galician landscape and village

---

[1] Jiri Langer, *Nine Gates to the Chassidic Mysteries*, Trans. Stephen Jolly, New York: David McKay Company, 1961: 4,6.

culture, but the Belz splendor and appreciation of the sounds of *davvenen* and *niggunim* remain:

> The Belz synagogue in Jerusalem is huge. Situated at the edge of Jerusalem, you can see it from afar as you come up from Tel Aviv. It looks like a fortress, like the original *shul* in Belz, but much larger. They say, "When *mashiah* will come, he'll see that *shul* first!" The acoustics there are so fantastic (because they will not permit any amplification). So you can imagine the wonderful sound those acoustics are capable of producing as 5,000 people *davven* together!

Galicianer Table-Banger I*

Syllabic Vocals: (Variable).
Source: Shlomo HaKohen Schachter, Vienna, Austria, ca. 1930s.
Origin: Galicia.

GALICIA IS AN AREA in the western Ukraine, the southern portion of which was the birthplace of Hasidism. The cities and towns in which the Ba'al Shem Tov lived and was first active in disseminating Hasidism were all in southern Galicia, a region called Podolia near the Carpathian Mountains. In these melodies, the spirit of that place, and the origins of Hasidism are preserved.

This *niggun* is especially suitable for singing at the table for the *Shabbat* noon meal.

Galicianer Table-Banger II *

Syllabic Vocals: (Variable).
Source: Shlomo HaKohen Schachter, Vienna, Austria, ca. 1930s.
Origin: Galicia.

---

* Original key C#m (capo 4).

33

IN THE 1960s, Reb Zalman began to frequent the *tish* (table) of Rabbi Shlomo Halberstam (1907-2000), the Bobover Rebbe. He was still loyal to HaBaD-Lubavitch, but was also attracted to the beauty and the deep aesthetic of Bobov. So he eventually came to discuss the matter in a private interview with the Bobover Rebbe. Reb Zalman described it this way:

> As I entered, I found him still dressed in his beautiful holiday *(yontif)* clothes, because the day after a holiday *(isru-hag)* is honored as the weekday special enough to be next to a holiday. I hand him my *kvittel* in which I said: "I already have a Rebbe. I'm a Lubavitcher Hasid. However, I also feel good coming here, and I would like to do this with your permission. I don't want to feel like I'm coming to 'steal' from you. I only want to share the warmth with your permission."

> So he says to me, "One may have an apple tree that bears Macintosh apples; but if one grafts a sprig from a Golden Delicious apple tree to it, in time it will grow to be part of that tree and bear fruit also. And from the Golden Delicious branch will come Golden Delicious apples, and from the main tree branches will come Macintosh apples."[2]

> Then he assumed a very familiar manner of speech and said, "Your father is a Galicianer (a Hasid from the region of Galicia), is he not?"

> I said, "Yes."

> Then he mused, "Toss a stick in the air and

---

[2] In this case, the tree (Reb Zalman) is a Macintosh apple tree (HaBaD-Lubavitch) to which a sprig of a Golden Delicious apple tree (HaGaT-Bobov) has been grafted. When the tree blossoms, all the blossoms will look the same, but "by the fruits you shall know them."

it falls on its root!" In other words, the apple doesn't fall far from the tree—Bobov is a Hasidic lineage from Galicia. In Bobov, I was always called "Zalman Zholkiever," after the Galician town in which I was born.[3]

Rabbi Shlomo Halberstam of Bobov II.
Photo by Zalman Schachter, ca. 1962.

---

[3] From an unpublished manuscript by Netanel Miles-Yepez.

Galicianer Table-Banger III*

Syllabic Vocals: (Variable).
Source: Shlomo HaKohen Schachter, Vienna, Austria, ca. 1930s.
Origin: Galicia.

ACCORDING TO REB ZALMAN, there are two basic kinds of *niggunim:*

> One is the *tish niggun*, a slow, more searching *niggun*, often sung at the Rebbe's 'table.' And then there were others for more happy occasions. So when there was a *simhah* (joyous

---

* Written in its original key (no capo needed).

occasion), a celebration, calling up the groom, or just regular *Shabbes* when you were in a good mood, you would sing one of these 'table bangers.'

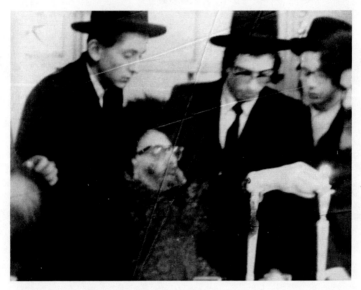

Rabbi Shlomo Halberstam of Bobov II. Photo by Zalman Schachter, ca. 1962.

Galicianer Table-Banger IV*

Syllabic Vocals: (Variable).
Source: Shlomo HaKohen Schachter, Vienna, Austria, ca. 1930s.
Origin: Galicia.

* Written in its original key (no capo needed). Form A A B A B C C B C
B.

WE ASKED REB ZALMAN, "What is the difference between Galicianer *niggunim* and those of other regions?"

I would say the difference between a Galicianer *niggun* and *niggunim* from other regions is like the difference between the third and the fourth chakras [of the Hindu Kundalini system]. Galicianer *niggunim* are very third *chakra niggunim*, they make you feel good in the belly, as it were; most of them are not much into the longing.

Rabbi Bentzion Halberstam of Bobov (1874-1941) and his son, Rabbi Shlomo Halberstam of Bobov (1907-2000).

Section II
Melodies and Songs of the Oiseh Hesed Shtibel in Vienna

THE OISEH HESED[4] *SHTIBEL* was the prayer-house of the Hasidic *hevra kadishah* (holy fellowship) who prepared the bodies of Hasidic families for burial in Vienna. Reb Zalman's father, Shlomo Schachter, was a *kohen* (of the priestly caste) and could not have actual contact with the bodies, but he found a way to participate in the *mitzvah* by keeping the books and the records of the fellowship. Thus, he too prayed in this *shtibel*. As Reb Zalman began to near *bar mitzvah*, his father began to take him more and more frequently to *davven* at the Oiseh Hesed *shtibel* where he heard many of these Hasidic songs and melodies. The Oiseh Hesed *shtibel* was a place were Hasidim of different Hasidic lineages davvened together, so it was a kind of crossroads of Hasidic *niggunim*, where *niggunim* from many different regions could be heard.

---

[4] This means, "those who act from true kindness," for they do a kindness for which there is no repayment, as it is done for the dead. The dead cannot give back anything in this world, so it is considered a special *mitzvah*.

*Avrumtche Geiger's March**

Syllabic Vocals: (Variable) though it may be sung to *El Adon* or *Kedusha*.
Composer: Avraham ("Avrumtche") Geiger, Vienna, Austria, ca. 1930s.
Source: Avraham Geiger, Oiseh Hesed *shtibel*, 2nd Precinct, Vienna,
Austria, ca. 1938.

AVRAHAM "AVRUMTCHE" GEIGER was the president
of the *hevra kadishah* of the Oiseh Hesed *shtibel* and had

---

* Original key Bm (capo 2). Has an improvised mid section – ad lib on
repeats.

once been the *gabbai* (attendant) of the Bluzhever Rebbe, Rabbi Tzvi Elimelekh Spira of Bluzhov (1841-1924).[5] Reb Zalman had this to say of him and his "march":

> Avrumtche Geiger was a wonderful character. I remember he had a broad face and a beautiful beard, and always had a big smile. I remember so many people from that time with dour features, but not him. It's funny, Reb Arele Roth, who was also a disciple of the Bluzhover Rebbe, described Avrumtche Geiger as being sort of 'tough,' a strong 'gatekeeper' *(gabbai)* for the Bluzhover. That was probably what he needed to be in that role, but I never saw him in this way.
>
> In Bluzhov, they didn't call him "Reb Avrumtche" like we did, but *Der Geiger*, 'the Geiger,' which shows that he probably was tough, or at least a little stern with Hasidim who came to eat-up the Rebbe's time. Before becoming a Hasid (and eventually the 'door' for the Rebbe), Reb Avrumtche had come from a more German environment, as shows from the name Geiger, which means 'violinist' in German, and was probably from the same family as Rabbi Abraham Geiger, the first Reform rabbi in Germany.
>
> After the Bluzhever Rebbe passed on, Reb Avrumtche settled in Vienna and became the head of the Hasidic *hevra kadishah*. At that time, there was an official *hevra kadishah* for the Jewish community of Vienna, and a separate group

---

[5] The Bluzhover Rebbe was the grandson of Rabbi Tzvi Elimelekh of Dinov (the B'nai Yissakhar), and a student of both Rabbi Hayyim of Tzanz and Rabbi Yehoshua of Belz.

for the Hasidic families. But when the official Jewish community had some problem, and public health was endangered, then he and his people would step in to take up the slack. Once, I remember, he received a medal from the Jewish community because of the remarkable job his group had done in just such an instance.

Reb Avrumtche also led the *davvenen* (prayers) at the Oiseh Hesed *Shtibel* and liked these Souza-type marches. This *niggun* of his always reminded me of a melody stolen from the marching band for the emperor, so I call it "Avrumtsche Geiger's March."[6]

---

[6] From an unpublished manuscript by Netanel Miles-Yepez.

Yidden In Einem *

Lyrics & Syllabic Vocals: (Yiddish)
Composer: Poss. Avraham Geiger, Vienna, Austria, ca. 1930s.
Source: Avraham Geiger, Oiseh Hesed *shtibel*, Vienna, Austria, ca. 1938.
Origin: Possibly a *niggun* of the Bluzhever Hasidim.

---

* Written in its original key (no capo needed).

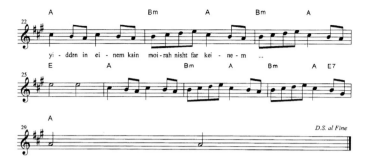

yi - dden in ei - nem kain moi-rah nisht far kei - ne - m ...

'Jews All Together'

THIS *NIGGUN* has an interesting anecdote attached to it that says a lot about Reb Avrumtche as a Hasid. Reb Zalman remembers it like this:

> Once, while on his way home early in the morning after a long session, Reb Avrumtche was accosted by some criminals who wanted to rob him and beat him up. He didn't have any money because it was *Shabbes*, so they started to threaten him. What could he do? He decided to dance with them and began singing, *Yidden in einem kain moirah nisht far keinem* . . . "Jews, all together, there's no reason to fear anyone except God. Let's be happy, let's rejoice, and throw out the night until the day arrives!" They must of thought he was crazy because they let him go![7]

---

[7] From an unpublished manuscript by Netanel Miles-Yepez.

The Balkan Dance*

Syllabic Vocals: (Variable).
Source: The Oiseh Hesed *Shtibel*, Vienna, Austria, *Simhat Torah*, ca. 1938.
Origin: Possibly the Balkan Peninsula.

---

* Written in its original key (no capo needed).

REB ZALMAN CALLS this upbeat *niggun* "The Balkan Dance," believing that its origins might be traced back to the Balkan Peninsula of Southeastern Europe, encompassing Greece, Croatia, Serbia, Yugoslavia, Bosnia, and Bulgaria.

Reb Zalman first heard this *niggun* in the Oiseh Hesed *shtibel* in the 2nd Precinct of Vienna known as "Matzah Island" on *Simhat Torah*, around 1938. On this occasion he remembers dancing to the *niggun* for hours with his father and the other Hasidim of the *shtibel*. But he also remembers hearing the very same *niggun* years later in a much different context:

Once, when visiting my friend David Jackson in Chicago, he took my sister Devorah and I out to eat at a Greek restaurant. The restaurant was one of those places that also had a band playing traditional Greek music while a belly-dancer danced for the people. And so when they saw my sister and me, they wanted to play us music to get us to dance too. To my great surprise, they began to play the Balkan dance *niggun* I had learned in Vienna! But since that didn't get us to get up on the dance floor, they decided to play *Hava Nagila* (Let us rejoice, a Hebrew folk song). So Devorah and I got up and danced with a handkerchief and they threw dollar bills at us!

Hungarian Gypsy Tune
for Dror Yïkra*

Lyrics & Syllabic Vocals: (Hebrew/Variable) *Dror Yïkra* of Dunash ibn
Labrat (920-990)
Source: Shlomo HaKohen Schachter, Oiseh Hesed *shtibel*, Vienna,
Austria, ca. 1938.
Origin: Possibly a Hungarian Gypsy Tune.

'Let Freedom Ring'

REB ZALMAN first heard this *niggun* from his father,
Shlomo Schachter. Of it, he says:

> My Papa used to sing that *niggun*. I liked it
> because I could almost see the band playing it.
> [Sings and gestures as if with cymbals] We used
> to sing it with a lot of harmony, that one. *Dror*

---

* Written in its original key (no capo needed). This piece goes into a free
form melody and then back to the original meter.

51

Yikra is a poem by Dunush ibn Labrat from the Spanish Golden Age, but I suspect it is a Hungarian gypsy tune, one that Brahms didn't include in his *Hungarian Dances*.

Dunash ibn Labrat (920-990 C.E.) was born in Fez, Morocco, and was a student of Rabbi Saadia Gaon. He is well-known as a biblical commentator, poet, and grammarian of the Golden Age of Jewish culture in Spain. In English translation, the words to his *Dror Yikra* are:

He will proclaim freedom for all his children
And will keep you as the apple of his eye
Pleasant is your name and will not be destroyed
Repose and rest on the Sabbath day.

Seek my sanctuary and my home.
Give me a sign of deliverance.
Plant a vine in my vineyard.
Look to my people, hear their laments.

Tread the wine-press in Bozrah,
And in Babylon that city of might
Crush my enemies in anger and fury.
On the day when I cry, hear my voice.

Plant, Oh God, in the mountain waste
Fir and acacia, myrtle and elm
Give those who teach and those who obey
Abundance peace, like the flow of a river.

Repel my enemies, Oh zealous God.
Fill their hearts with fear and despair.
Then we shall open our mouths,
And fill our tongues with Your praise.

Know wisdom, that your soul may live,
And it shall be a diadem for your brow.
Keep the commandment of your Holy One
Observe the Sabbath, your sacred day.

Nïkolsburg Nïggun*

Syllabic Vocals: (Variable).
Source: Hasidim of the Oiseh Hesed *Shtibel*, 2nd Precinct, Vienna,
Austria, *Simhat Torah*, ca. 1938.
Origin: Possibly from Moravia.

REB ZALMAN says of this *niggun:*

> This *niggun* is often attributed to the Ba'al Shem
> Tov, but I don't believe it. However, it is also
> said that it was sung at the court of Shmelke
> [Horowitz] of Nikolsburg [1726-1778]. And
> since I first heard it in my junior high
> *[Gymnasium]* from a visiting music teacher who
> was Moravian, and since the *niggun* wasn't from

---

* Written in its original key (no capo needed).

55

Galicia, I figured it was from Nikolsburg in Moravia . . . It is a conclusion. You know, when you don't have musical notation, how do you remember a *niggun*? You give it a "filename." So I call it the "Nikolsburg Niggun."

Niggun Waltz from Burgenland[*]

Syllabic Vocals: (Variable).
Source: Hasidim of the Oiseh Hesed *Shtibel*, 2nd Precinct, Vienna,
Austria, *Simhat Torah*, ca. 1938.
Origin: Burgenland.

---

* Original key Bbm (capo 1). Used for *Shir ha'Ma'alot*.

REB ZALMAN says of this *niggun:*

Burgenland is a province of Austria adjacent to Hungary. The Jews who lived there were not quite Hasidic Jews, but liked to have Hasidic rabbis who were strong and spirited. They didn't quite recognize the boundaries because of how they were situated geographically. In the Austro-Hungarian Empire, Burgenland had towns with Hungarian names and others with German names, so they were clearly between these cultures in many ways.

Section III

Melodies and Songs from the Vizhnitz Shtibel in Antwerp

AFTER THE SCHACHTER family escaped from Austria in 1938, they made their way to Antwerp, Belgium. There, Reb Zalman's father and he would go various places to *davven*, one of which was the prayer-house of the Vizhnitzer Hasidim.

Vizhnitz Simhat Torah Dance *

Syllabic Vocals: (Variable).
Source: Vizhnitzer Hasidim, Vienna, Austria, 1936.
Origin: A *niggun* of the Vizhnitzer Hasidim.

---

* Original key is Bbm one half step higher (capo 1).

REB ZALMAN actually heard this for the first time in 1936, in Vienna, Austria. The Vizhnitzer Rebbe, Israel Hager of Vizhnitz (1860-1936) was walking down the street and his Hasidim were singing this melody. Later, in Antwerp, in the Vizhnitzer *Shtibel* on Simhat Torah, he heard it again.

Vizhnitz Hakafot Dance*

Syllabic Vocals: (Variable).
Source: Vizhnitzer Shtibel, Antwerp, Belgium, ca.1938.
Origin: A *niggun* of the Vizhnitzer Hasidim.

AFTER THE SIMHAT TORAH DANCE, Reb Zalman says
the Vizhnitzer Hasidim sang this melody.

---

* Original key is Ebm (capo 1).

63

Section IV

Melodies and Songs of the "Diamond-Cutters" in Antwerp

WHILE STILL IN ANTWERP, Belgium, a fourteen-year-old Zalman Schachter came into contact with a small circle of HaBaD Hasidim (of the now extinct Niezhin and Kopusht lineages) who worked together cutting and polishing diamonds. Though he had grown up in a Hasidic family, it wasn't until he met the "Diamond-Cutters" that he was truly initiated into Hasidic ways of thinking and living.

Passport photo of a young Zalman Schachter.

Hokhmat Adam Tair Panav*

Syllabic Vocals & Lyrics: (Variable/Hebrew).
Composer: Shneur Zalman of Liadi (1745-1812), White Russia.
Source: Barukh Merzel, Antwerp, Belgium, ca. 1940.
Origin: HaBaD-Niezhin or HaBaD-Kopusht Lineage.

---

* Written in its original key (no capo needed). Transcribed by Hazzan
Richard Kaplan.

'The Wisdom of a Person Gives Light to the Face'

THIS *NIGGUN* IS ONE of the most precious in this collection. It is reported to be a *niggun* of Rabbi Shneur Zalman of Liadi (1745-1812), the Alter Rebbe, founder of HaBaD Hasidism, transmitted through the oral traditions of the now extinct lineages of HaBaD-Niezhin and Kopusht. Today, only HaBaD-Lubavitch is still existing, and this *niggun* is not among their standard collections.

Of it, Reb Zalman says:

> I learned this *niggun* from Reb Barukh Merzel, who learned it from Reb Moshe Chekhoval, of blessed memory. They were my first mentors in HaBaD Hasidism and they gave this over as a *niggun* of the Alter Rebbe, who loved that verse, "The Wisdom of a person gives light to the face" (Ecclesiastes 8:1).[8] It came through the Kopushter[9] line to Reb Avrohom Schneersohn, who was the father in law of my Rebbe, and Rav Tzirelsohn, the rabbi of Kishinev, to Reb Moshe, who received it from them. We would sing this when we got to serious *niggunim*, when we wanted to learn or meditate.

---

[8] In the liner notes to his CD *Le Chayim–To Life*, Reb Zalman translates the title as, 'Wisdom's Shining Face' and then commented, "The union of the sage and Sofia brings light."

[9] For reasons not necessary to go into here, Reb Zalman includes Niezhin in Kopushter HaBaD.

Ze HaKodesh*

Syllabic Vocals & Lyrics: (Variable/Hebrew) Unknown Israeli or Hebrew Poet.
Source: Barukh Merzel and the "Diamond Cutter" Hevrah, Antwerp, Belgium, ca. 1940.

'This Holy'

REB ZALMAN LEARNED this *Seudah Shlishit* ('third meal') *niggun* from Reb Barukh Merzel and the "Diamond Cutter" *hevrah* in Antwerp, Belgium. Of it, Reb Zalman says:

---

* Original key Cm (capo 3).

This *niggun* can be sung as a round. The ending line was sung with the Hebrew, *Lama lo natata li mi'ze hakodesh pa'amayim bashavua?* "Why did you not grant of this holy twice a week?" You see, "holy" is a noun in this context of what comes before, when it says, "May the *Shabbat* rest of Israel give us freedom and deep repose," but then it goes on, "But there is just one complaint that I have; why did you not grant of *this holy* twice a week?"

A Gantz Yohr Freylach*

Syllabic Vocals & Lyrics: (Variable/Yiddish).
Source: Barukh Merzel and the "Diamond Cutter" Hevrah,
Antwerp, Belgium, ca. 1940.
Origin: Traditional.

---

* Written in its original key (no capo needed).

'All Year Happy'

REB ZALMAN REMEMBERS dancing to the tune of *A Gantz Yohr Freylah!* ('all year happy!') for two hours straight on Purim with the "Diamond Cutter" *hevrah* ('fellowship'), smoking cigars and drinking mulled wine.

Rabbi Zalman Schachter reunited with Shlomo Rosenfeld (2nd and 3rd from left) of the "Diamond-Cutters" at Yeshivat HaBaD Lod in 1958.

Modzhitz Dance*

Syllabic Vocals: (Variable).
Source: Barukh Merzel and the "Diamond Cutter" Hevrah, Antwerp, Belgium, ca. 1939.
Origin: Modzhitzer Hasidim, Demblin (Modzhitz), Poland.

REB ZALMAN FIRST learned this *niggun* in Antwerp in 1939. It is a *niggun* of the Modzhitzer Hasidim, whose founder, Reb Yisrael Taub (1849-1921) made music

---

* Written in its original key (no capo needed).

the major emphasis of Modzhitz Hasidim, and among whom it became an art form. The Modzhitzer Hasidim have numerous marches, dances, and contemplative *niggunim*.

Reb Zalman remembers:

They sometimes sang this in Lubavitch [in Brooklyn] also. I remember playing this on my recorder at a *farbrengen* [celebratory gathering] at which the Rebbe, Reb Yosef Yitzhak [Schneersohn, the 6th Lubavitcher Rebbe] was present. Unfortunately I was in the back and couldn't see how he was reacting to it. Later, I used to play this *niggun* on my clarinet at different Lubavitch weddings.

Section V

Melodies and Songs of the Hasidim in Brooklyn

REB ZALMAN SAYS of the *niggunim* of this period:

When I first came to America and entered the HaBaD-Lubavitch *yeshiva*, there were very few 'born Habadnikes' around.

Many of the people who were associated with HaBaD in Brooklyn in those days were immigrants who, in Europe, were attached to other Hasidic lineages; so many *niggunim* that were floating around HaBaD at that time came from non-HaBaD sources. For instance, all the Hechts, a big HaBaD family now, are descended from Shia Hecht, and so there was Moishe Hecht, Yankel Hecht, Peretz Hecht, and Sholem Hecht, and all these Hechtelach had 'become Habadnikes.' Yankel Hecht had a good voice and he had learned how to be a *ba'al tefilliah* [prayer leader] the Galicianer way. Then there was Berel Baumgarten who came in from the Vorke group. There was also Velvel Schildkraut, who came from someplace in Williamsburg. In those days, there were also the *Malokhim*, the break-away HaBaD group, under a disciple of Reb Shalom Dov Baer of Lubavitch who felt that HaBaD had gotten too worldly, and they too knew some special *niggunim*.

So though I was now a Habadnik, I was learning *niggunim* from all over the place.

75

Modzhitz March[*]

Syllabic Vocals: (Variable).
Source: Shaul Yedidyah Elazar Taub (1882-1947), Williamsburg,
Brooklyn, New York, ca. 1946.
Origin: Modzhitzer Hasidim, Demblin (Modzhitz), Poland.

---

[*] Original key C# (capo 1).

REB ZALMAN ONCE went to visit the Modzhitzer Rebbe, Rabbi Shaul Yedidyah Elazar Taub of Modzhitz (1882-1947) in Williamsburg, Brooklyn with his friend Avraham Weingarten while they were studying in the *yeshiva* together. At that time, they heard the Modzhitzer Rebbe sing this at a *tish* ('table' gathering).

Zalman Schachter as a yeshiva *bokher* in Lubavitch.

Makarever Niggun*

Syllabic Vocals: (Variable).
Source: Samuel Resnick, Brooklyn, New York, ca. 1940s.
Origin: Makarever Hasidim, Makarav, Ukraine, ca. 1800.

nai   nai   nai   nai   ...

---

* Written in its original key (no capo needed).

REB ZALMAN DISCUSSED the possible origins of this *niggun* with us, saying:

> I first heard this *niggun* in Lubavitch, but they don't sing it often there. Why was it sung in Lubavitch? Because it is of a contemplative kind. However, I also heard it from my first father-in-law, Samuel Resnik, who was a Ukranian Jew, and whose family would visit Reb Moshe Mordechai of Makarav, a Rebbe of the Twersky-Chernobyle dynasty. Later, I asked Mordechai Twersky [the Hornesteipler Rebbe of Denver] about this *niggun*, but he didn't know it as a Twersky *niggun*, he thought it was a Karliner *niggun*.

Zalman Schachter as a young Lubavitch emissary.

Melodies and Songs of HaBaD Hasidism

THESE FOUR *NIGGUNIM* are just a small sampling of the many great *niggunim* of HaBaD Hasidism. *Hokhmat Adam Tair Panav* is reprinted here in order to return it to its proper context, as it has been lost to HaBaD Hasidism for many years. Included with it is a *niggun* of the third Rebbe of HaBaD, Menachem Mendel of Lubavitch I, and two favorites of the fifth and sixth Lubavitcher Rebbes.

A HaBaD-Lubavitch *farbrengen* with Rabbi Menachem Mendel Schneerson of Lubavitch II (1902-1994). Zalman Schachter, ca. 1960.

Hokhmat Adam Tair Panav*

Syllabic Vocals & Lyrics: (Variable / Hebrew).
Composer: Shneur Zalman of Liadi (1745-1812), White Russia.
Source: Barukh Merzel, Antwerp, Belgium, ca. 1940.
Origin: HaBaD-Niezhin or HaBaD-Kopusht Lineage.

---

* Written in its original key (no capo needed). Transcribed by Hazzan
Richard Kaplan.

'The Wisdom of a Person Gives Light to the Face'

THIS *NIGGUN* IS ONE of the most precious in this collection. It is reported to be a *niggun* of Rabbi Shneur Zalman of Liadi (1745-1812), the Alter Rebbe, founder of HaBaD Hasidism, transmitted through the oral traditions of the now extinct lineages of HaBaD-Niezhin and Kopusht. Today, only HaBaD-Lubavitch is still existing, and this *niggun* is not among their known collections. It is also included in Section IV because of the source from which Reb Zalman learned it. More of its story can be read in that section.

Rabbi Shneur Zalman of Liadi (1745-1812)

The D'veiqut Niggun of the Tzemah Tzedek*

Syllabic Vocals: (Variable).
Composer: Menachem Mendel Schneersohn of Lubavitch I (1789-1866), White Russia, ca. 1850.

---

* Written in original key (A minor, as on the recording). Transcribed by Hazzan Richard Kaplan.

'In Loving Touch Melody'

THIS CONTEMPLATIVE *NIGGUN,* in the Wallachian (Rumanian) mode, was composed by Rabbi Menachem Mendel of Lubavitch I (1789-1866), the 3rd Lubavitcher Rebbe, called the Tzemah Tzedek. Reb Zalman tells us that it was called, "The Tzemah Tzedek's *D'veikut,*" which he translates as 'In Loving Touch With God.' Elsewhere he has written:

The word *[D'veikut]* is from the noun *[DBK]* which means glue, cement; it is a synonym with the word whose root *TFL*, from which *Tefillah*, prayer, is derived as in '*Tofel Kli Heres*'— mending an earthen vessel. *[DBK]* means "Being in touch." [. . .] The natural state is to be in *[D'veikut]*. The practice of *[D'veikut]* is to affirm that a state of grace, of 'not two,' is always present.

Since *[D'veikut]* is close to the unitive but not identical with it, it may be said that it corresponds to the relationship of Light with Lumen, the self-effulgent source of Light. This also implies a sense of '*Bittul*,' effacement, of the one who is in *[D'veikut]*. It is rather a joyous wiliness to be transparent, to be the vehicle for the light. Here resides a deep bliss with tinges of awesomeness.[10]

---

[10] Zalman Schachter-Shalomi. *Gate to the Heart: An Evolving Process*. Philadelphia: 1993: 24-25.

Rabbi Menachem Mendel of Lubavitch I (1789-1866),
the 3rd Lubavitcher Rebbe, called the Tzemah Tzedek.

The Hakhonoh Niggun *

Syllabic Vocals & Lyrics: (Variable/English) "The Rebbe's Preparatory Song" by Zalman Schachter (ca. 1952).
Composer: A HaBaD Hasid.
Source: HaBaD-Lubavitcher Hasidim, Crown Heights, Brooklyn, New York, 1940s.

---

* Original key is Bbm one half step higher (capo 1).

THIS *NIGGUN* was especially loved by Rabbi Shalom Dov Baer Schneersohn of Lubavitch (1860-1920), the 5th Lubavitcher Rebbe, who would sing it before delivering a *ma'amar* (Hasidic discourse).

This is also one of three traditional *niggunim* for which Reb Zalman composed English lyrics in order that his students would be able to understand the "conscious content" of the *niggun*. Here are the lyrics as he originally composed them:

The Rebbe's Preparatory Song

For the sake of my soul, I search for a goal,

And I find none other than Thee, O Lord.

Thou find'st satisfaction in our mitzvah *action,*

If Thy light in Thy Torah we see.

O grant me the awareness, of Thy so precious nearness,

In Thy presence, O Lord, I long to dwell;
Help me from the start to make pure my heart
And all in the end will turn out well.

O Lord, so many years have gone by in great waste,
'Til of Thy wondrous sweetness
Thou has granted me a taste;
Reach me please and teach me,
And keep me in Thy Grace
Until the day in which I may see Thy holy face. [11]

---

[11] Zalman Schachter-Shalomi. *Hashir V'hashevah: The Song and the Praise*: 13. In the past, Reb Zalman has sometimes called this "The Rostov Niggun," and his lyrics, "The Rebbe's Rostov Song," but this *niggun* is now clearly identified as the *Hakhonoh Niggun*.

Rabbi Shalom Dov Baer Schneersohn of Lubavitch,
5th Lubavitcher Rebbe (1860-1920)

The Beinoni Niggun*

Syllabic Vocals: (Variable).
Composer: Ahron Haritonov of Nikolayev, a HaBaD Hasid.
Source: HaBaD-Lubavitcher Hasidim, Crown Heights, Brooklyn, New York, 1940s.

___

* Original key is one half step lower (tune guitar down 1/2 step).

'The Betweener Melody'

IN *SEFER HANIGGUNIM*, Rabbi Samuel Zalmonoff describes the history of this *niggun* (in Reb Zalman's own free translation):

> Reb Ahron Haritonov [a *shohet* and HaBaD hasid who composed a number of HaBaD *niggunim*] came from Nikolayev. The Rebbe, Reb Yosef Yitzhak [Schneersohn of Lubavitch, 6th Lubavitcher Rebbe, 1880-1950], liked this *niggun* a great deal and called it "The Beynoni," because it described the *beynoni* [by way of a melody] just as the *Tanya* does [with words].[12]
>
> The movements of this *niggun* are very, very special. It does not have the usual aesthetic of music, but expresses the feeling of the heart and the expression of the soul reaching toward the Infinite. In other words, the movements of this *niggun* transcend the domain of the regular music and approach the kind of speech the soul can utter without words. They go up and down, demanding and seeking, and you cannot help but close your eyes when you sing this

---

[12] It is known that Reb Shalom Baer Schneersohn of Lubavitch, 5th Lubavitcher Rebbe (1860-1920) also loved this *niggun*.

niggun, focusing your mind and your heart. "The Beynoni" carries in itself a whole treasure of soul and poetry. No wonder the Rebbe liked it so much.

Reb Zalman remembers one particular singing of this *niggun* vividly:

My Rebbe, Reb Yosef Yitzhak [of Lubavitch], once asked that we should sing that *niggun* during a *farbrengen* [gathering] in the upstairs dining room (where he often held his *farbrengens*). And so it happened that the person who was leading the singing began to speed it up—and I never saw the Rebbe get so tough as he did then—the Rebbe banged his fist on the table and said, "I won't have you spoil this for me . . . Who gave you the right to put your mind on the next note when you're still singing this one?" And so he took us back and we sang "The Beynoni" all over again, but this time with more soul.

Rabbi Yosef Yitzhak Schneersohn (1880-1950), the 6th Lubavitcher Rebbe on board the ship which brought him to America.

Section VII
Melodies and Songs of the Early Hasidic Rebbes

Niggun of the Ba'al Shem Tov[*]

Syllabic Vocals & Lyrics: (Variable/English) "The BeShT's Song"
by Zalman Schachter (ca. 1952).
Composer: Israel ben Eleazar Tallismacher, Ba'al Shem Tov
(ca.1698-1760).

---

[*] Written in original key.

IN *THE LIGHT AND FIRE of the Baal Shem Tov*, Maggid Yitzhak Buxbaum writes:

> The Baal Shem Tov was a gifted singer with an expressive voice. He considered singing a service to God, for music touches the soul and produces an outpouring of the soul. He often led his disciples in song, especially at the Sabbath table. Sometimes he asked them to close their eyes and put their hands on each other's shoulders as they sang, so that they were all connected in a sacred circle. He used to say, "When you put your hand on your brother's shoulder, you physically express your resolve to fulfill the commandment to love your neighbor as yourself."[13]

---

[13] Yitzhak Buxbaum. *The Light and Fire of the Baal Shem Tov*. New York: Continuum, 2005: 150-51.

When Reb Zalman first began to teach this *niggun* during his visits to college campuses in the late 1940s, he noticed that often the students who sang along were merely trying to reproduce the sounds, but clearly had no idea about the "conscious content" behind the sounds. So in order to give them some idea of the meaning and emotion behind the music, Reb Zalman composed these English lyrics for it.

The BeShT's Song

As I sit, and I sing,
  I remember my heavenly home;
As I sit, and I think,
  I feel the nearness of God's throne;
Lord, my light, heart's delight,
  Thee I seek, Thee alone.

Thy sweet love, O God above,
  Thrills me, fills me, gives me life;
With Thy power, my Rock and Tower,
  Thy Will to do I'll strive.

The ray-s of Gra-ce Thy To-rah ra-di-ate-s!
  Guide me on the road, to Thine heavenly abode;
Thy Wisdom bright, Understanding's light,
  In Knowledge will abide.

O-h Lor-d! lift my earthly load,
  Guide me on the road, to Thine heavenly abode;
Thy Wisdom bright, Understanding's light,
  In Knowledge will abide.

Thy sweet love, O God above,
    Thrills me, fills me, gives me life;
  With Thy power, my Rock and Tower,
    Thy Will to do I'll strive . . .[14]

Reb Zalman adds:

> When I presented these lyrics to the Rebbe,
> Reb Menachem Mendel [Schneerson of
> Lubavitch, 7th Lubavitcher Rebbe, 1902-1994],
> he agreed that these words fit the feeling of the
> melody.[15]

---

[14] Zalman Schachter-Shalomi. *Hashir V'hashevah: The Song and the Praise*: 12.
As the *niggun* does not have a discrete ending, the lyrics do not either.

[15] During that same meeting with the Rebbe, Reb Zalman also presented
the lyrics he had written to the "Hakhonoh Niggun" and the "Niggun of
Reb Mikeleh Zlotchover." The Rebbe endorsed these as well.

Mikeleh of Zlotchov's Melody Stirring and Inciting Divine Mercy

Syllabic Vocals & Lyrics: (Variable/English) "Reb Yosef Yitzhak's Song" by Zalman Schachter (ca. 1952). Composer: Yehiel Mikeleh of Zlotchov (ca. 1731-1786).[16]

AS THE DISCIPLES of the holy Ba'al Shem Tov gathered around his deathbed, he motioned to them to come nearer. They leaned close to hear what he might need. Then he said to them, "Please let me hear the *niggun* of Mikeleh of Zlotchov," which the Ba'al Shem Tov had named, "the melody that stirs and incites divine mercy."

When his disciples had finished singing the *niggun*, the Ba'al Shem Tov said to them:

> *I guarantee you for all generations, that no matter when, whosoever shall sing this melody with a stir of contrition* (t'shuvah), *wherever I shall be I shall hear it—for there are angels that bring messages to the souls—and I*

---

[16] These slower *niggunim*, expressive of great longing, are exceptionally difficult to transcribe into musical notation. I have made honest attempts with most of these, but the subtleties of Reb Mikeleh of Zlotchov's *niggun* have resisted accurate transcription. Therefore, I recommend that one who wishes to learn this *niggun* listen to the recording provided on the *At the Rebbe's Table* CD and sing along with it again and again until it has been completely absorbed. — E.R.

shall sing along and incite Divine Compassion for the contrite singer.[17]

This is the third *niggun* in this volume for which Reb Zalman wrote special lyrics in English. As Reb Zalman first heard the story of the three-part composition of this *niggun* from his Rebbe, Reb Yosef Yitzhak of Lubavitch (1880-1950), his lyrics refer to the final message of Reb Yosef Yitzhak to his Hasidim, and in this way, the lyrics and melody are meant to bring together the Ba'al Shem Tov and Reb Yosef Yitzhak of Lubavitch as prayer partners for whoever might be singing the *niggun*.

Reb Yosef Yitzhak's Song

I came to my garden
From beyond time and space
To meet my bride, my beloved
At our special meeting place,
For not the angels of Heaven above
But you, my soul I love.

My Lord, my Love, My Groom,
With Thee let me commune;
Please regard
That in my heart
For Thee I have made a room.

My Lord, my Love, My Groom,
Please save me from doom

[17] J. I. Schochet. *Rabbi Israel Baal Shem Tov: A monograph on the Life and Teachings of the Founder of Chassidism.* Toronto: Lieberman Publishing House, 1961: 113,116-117.

I shall heed
      Thy word in deed
In joy, but never in gloom.

Save my soul from evil's rule,
      It makes one act just like a fool;
So that the truth I'll realize
      And follow Thee, O Eternally Wise.

To see then clear, just how ideal
      It is for me, Thee near to feel
So hear my Lord, do hear my sigh
      With Torah, Turning, and Right acts
To Thee my knot I tie.[18]

---

[18] Zalman Schachter-Shalomi. *Hashir V'hashevah: The Song and the Praise*: 12.

Yah Ekhsof Noam Shabbat of Ahron of Karlin I*

Syllabic Vocals & Lyrics: (Variable/English) *Yah Ekhsof Noam Shabbat* translated by Zalman Schachter-Shalomi.
Composer: Ahron ben Ya'akov Perlow, the Great of Karlin (1736-1772).

REB ZALMAN SAYS of this *niggun:*

> This is a great *niggun* of longing. We know that Ahron of Karlin I composed this in the lifetime of his *rebbe*, the Maggid of Mezritch, because Reb Ahron died before the Maggid [the same year]. And he also made a poem called, *Yah Ekhsof Noam Shabbat*, "Oh God, How I Long for the *Shabbat*" and I translated this into English.
>
> Reb Ahron's version is hard to sing in Hebrew because it doesn't have any rhyme or

---

* * Original key Fm (capo 1). Transcribed by Hazzan Richard Kaplan.

rhythm to it. So I set it to a rhyme and a rhythm in English so that it could be sung to this melody of his that I first heard in Lubavitch.

Yah! How I long for the bliss of the Shabbat,
united in secret with Your own fervent wish.
Give way to Your own deep desire to love us.
May Sabbath in Torah be our sacred bliss.
Share Her with us who desire to please You—
Our deep thirst for union be met with delight.

Holy Presence that fills time and space!
Keep safe who keep Shabbat *in their longing all week.*
Like a deer that seeks water by the banks of the river,
We seek Shabbat, *the secret of Your sacred Name!*
Grant us all week long Her shimmering Presence,
So our hearts and our faith be pure service to You!

Warmly embrace us with Your kind compassion,
Quench quickly our thirst for Your unending Grace.
Give us the bliss drink from Eden's own river.
Your praises we sing with joy on our face.
Let Jacob's gift to us—echo all week long
Infusing our lives with a Shabbes-*filled trace.*

Hail Shabbat, *delight of our souls and our Spirits.*
Ecstasy life-throb I am awed by Your love,
Secure in Your caring there is safety and nurture—
You feed us sweet nectar from Your Source above.
As You embrace us with Mothering comfort—
In You I take refuge and pledge You my love.[19]

[19] Zalman Schachter-Shalomi. *Paradigm Shift: From the Jewish Renewal Teachings of Reb Zalman Schachter-Shalomi.* Northvale, New Jersey: Jason Aronson, 1993: 204.

Section VIII
A Modern Melody and Song of Neo-Hasidism

Rabbis Zalman Schachter-Shalomi, Shlomo Carlebach, and David Zeller
on stage in Bombay, India, 1982. Surya Green, 1982.

Lord I Want to Do For You*

Syllabic Vocals & Lyrics: (Variable/English) Zalman Schachter, Minneapolis, Minnesota, ca. 1969.
Composer: Shlomo Carlebach (1925-1994).

WE ASKED REB ZALMAN, "How did your words get together with Reb Shlomo's *niggun*?"

Very simple; I was teaching about the Four Worlds *[arba olamot]* in the early days of the House of Love and Prayer [in the Haight-

---

* Original key Bbm (capo 1).

Ashbury district of San Francisco] and I needed a carrier-wave for the teaching. I used this *niggun* because it grows that way [through the Worlds]. *Mi Kamokha* is what they call Shlomo's *niggun*, but it has changed from the way he first sung it and the way I sing it now.

Lord I Want To Do For You

Lord I want to Do for You.
Lord I want to Feel for You.
Lord I want to Know for You.
Lord I want to Be for You.

> *You are Action*
> *You are Feeling*
> *You are Knowledge*
> *You are Being.*

> *You are Action*
> *You are Feeling*
> *You are Knowledge*
> *You just Are.*

In 2002, a student of Reb Zalman's, Sigmond Kal Shore and his family were invited to have dinner with Pope John Paul II (Karol Jozef Wojtyla, 1920-2005) in the Papal Residence in Rome. His grandmother, Dr. Lena Allen-Shore, was a friend of the Pope's from Poland, and at that time, was working on a new edition of the book *Building Bridges: Pope John Paul II and the Horizons of Life* on their friendship. During the course of dinner, Pope John Paul II asked Kal, "What are the Jewish youth inspired by today?" Kal explained a little bit about the work of Reb Zalman and the heartfelt renewal of traditional Jewish practice with a modern sensibility. He then sang the Pope this Reb Shlomo *niggun* with Reb Zalman's lyrics in its entirety!

Biographies

Zalman Schachter-Shalomi, better known as 'Reb Zalman,' was born in Zholkiew, Poland, in 1924. His family fled the Nazi oppression in 1938 and finally landed in New York City in 1941. He was ordained by the Lubavitcher Hasidim in 1947. For fifty years, he has been considered one of the world's foremost teachers of Hasidism and Kabbalah. He is the father of the Jewish Renewal movement, the founder of the Spiritual Eldering Institute, and an active participant in ecumenical dialogues, including the widely influential dialogue with the Dalai Lama documented in the book *The Jew in the Lotus*. He is the author of *Wrapped in a Holy Flame: Teachings and Tales of the Hasidic Masters* (Jossey-Bass, 2003) and *Jewish with Feeling: Guide to a Meaningful Jewish Practice* (Riverhead, 2005). Reb Zalman currently lives in Boulder, Colorado.

Eyal Rivlin was born in the blistering heat of Israel's Jordan Valley, but his heart seems to spring from Renaissance Europe. His passion for celebrating music, dance, science, and spiritual growth led him from the Tel Aviv music scene on a pilgrimage of discovery through Europe and India to the United States, and a Master's Degree in Transpersonal Psychology. For years, Eyal played hide-and-seek with God, until finally learning to surrender to the Divine sound of each moment. Now, happily centered in Boulder Colorado, Eyal inspires joy through performing, teaching and facilitating musical events. His compositions and performances can be heard on Bat Kol's *PrayerSongs*, and along with Danya Uriel on their CD, *Coming Home*.

Netanel Miles-Yepez was born in Battle Creek, Michigan in 1972, and studied History of Religions at Michigan State University and Contemplative Religion at Naropa University, specializing in comparative religion and non-dual philosophies. He has been a personal student of Rabbi Zalman Schachter-Shalomi since 1998, and co-founded the Sufi-Hasidic, Inayati-Maimuni Order with him in 2004. He is co-author of *A Heart Afire: Stories and Teachings of the Early Hasidic Masters* (Jewish Publication Society, 2009) and *A Merciful God: Stories and Teachings of the Holy Rebbe, Levi Yitzhak of Berditchev* (Albion-Andalus, 2010). He lives in Boulder, Colorado, where he is a spiritual counselor, editor, and painter of religious icons.

Made in United States
North Haven, CT
17 December 2024

62738429R00071